Ladoo Dog: Tales of a Sweet Dachshund

Published by Aneeta Sundararaj

Copyright

Ladoo Dog: Tales of a
Copyright 2013 Aneeta Sundararaj

License Notes

This ebook is licensed for your personal enjoyment only. This ebook may not be re-sold or given away to other people. If you would like to share this book with another person, please purchase an additional copy for each recipient. If you're reading this book and did not purchase it, or it was not purchased for your use only, then please return to Amazon.com (Kindle) and purchase your own copy. Thank you for respecting the hard work of this author.

To read more of Aneeta's work, her website: http://www.howtotellagreatstory.com

Contents

Copyright 2
Contents 3
What Others Are Saying About Ladoo Dog 4
Dedication 6
Chapter 1: A Little about Dachshunds 9
Chapter 2: I Was Chosen 13
Chapter 3: An Indian Dog 21
Chapter 4: Ladoo and Her Ten Names 29
Chapter 5: Stretch Dog 37
Chapter 7: Ladoo Upstairs 50
Chapter 8: Ladoo and the Tsunami 58
Chapter 9: Dancing Kambing and Gambling 64
Chapter 10: Sound of a Heart Breaking 68
Chapter 11: Temper Tantrum 72
Chapter 12: Friday is a Good Day 79
Author's Note 87
Back Cover 90

What Others Are Saying About Ladoo Dog

In these stories, you'll read how Ladoo showed all the people she came into contact with the meaning of love and loyalty – for life. She and Aneeta clearly loved each other – soul to soul.

> Kathleen Rowley

Aneeta's dedication to and love for Ladoo tells us what we know in our hearts to be true, but often take for granted. Like a mother's hug, her work is warm and endearing. Thank you Aneeta, thank you Ladoo.

> G. Rajasingam

I sincerely believe that it is on account of Rinunabandha (former relationship) that Ladoo and Aneeta came together. This is a lovely account of a love between a 'mother' and her 'child'.

> Tan Sri Dato' Seri Azlanii Dr. M. Mahadevan

…Anyone who has enjoyed the companionship of the four-legged will be able to empathise and walk through the author's experiences as we discover the unconditional love of our pets and depths to ourselves which we may not otherwise have explored.

> Toh Puan Umasundari Sambanthan

This is a touching love story between a woman and a dog. It is no ordinary love. It's a mother's love - pure and undefiled. The law of attraction prevailed at the first encounter itself between the two - commonly termed as 'love at first sight'.

Datin Paduka Mother A Mangalam

The phrase 'They were made for each other' is quite commonly used; however, you only have to read this book to see a true example. Ladoo was a wonderful dog who not only gave herself heart and soul to Aneeta [and received the same in return] but also touched the souls of many other people with her amazing character.

Susan Keefe

… If ever I should be asked the question what do you want to return as, if you believe in reincarnation, I would unhesitatingly say to return as Ladoo with Aneeta as my mistress.

Merlyn Swan

Dedication

This book is for my mother, Sharayu Sundararaj. She believes that Ladoo must have done some good karma to have been loved this much. I feel the opposite is true: I must have done some good karma for the many blessings that my parents and this four-legged 'daughter' give me.

Chapter 1: A Little about Dachshunds

In the 15th century, the Germans started a selective breeding technique among several breeds of dogs. The aim of this experiment was to create a dog that was strong enough to hunt a badger, have the ability of a hound and the temperament of a terrier. Some 200 years later, the dog they created had an elongated head and body, a protruding sternum, short legs with unusually large and paddle-shaped paws, hound-type ears which hung down its cheeks, arched eyebrows set in a long muzzle and a robust jaw. This sturdy, well-muscled dog possessed confidence, courage bordering on recklessness and fought fearlessly with the badgers. They named the dog 'Dachshund'. The name of this new breed of dog is derived from two German words: 'Dachs' meaning 'badger' and 'hund' meaning 'dog'. Today, a Dachshund is also referred to as, 'Wiener Dog,' 'Sausage Dog' or even 'Doxie'.

Dachshunds come in two sizes: standard (between 10 and 15 kg) and miniature (between 5 and 10 kg).

Then, there are what I call 'Subsets of Dachshunds':

Long-haired Dachshunds: these docile dogs have a coat that is similar to an Irish Setter and the temperament of a spaniel.

Smooth-haired Dachshunds: they have a coat that is short, smooth and shining. Sometimes, smooth-haired Dachshunds can have coats that are a mixture of colours, but are generally red, cream, black and tan or chocolate. Ladoo was a smooth-haired standard dachshund.

Wire-haired Dachshunds – these dogs have coats that are wiry, short, thick and rough. With beards and bushy eyebrows, they can look very smart.

When the vet first met Ladoo, he said to me, "A dachshund is obsessively possessive of its master." How true. Ladoo certainly demonstrated that dachshunds can be very possessive of their master and are extremely jealous if affection is shown elsewhere. Even so, you will never be alone if you choose to keep a dachshund – wherever you go, you are sure to have a long, low shadow following you.

Though dachshunds are lively and affectionate, they are also proud, stubborn and tend to make their own decisions on any given matter. For example, a dachshund, known for making its own rules when playing games, might run after a ball and fetch it; however, it will not see the necessity to bring the ball back to you. Dachshunds are very good watchdogs, compulsive diggers and love to bark (sometimes unnecessarily). It is always a good idea to take your dachshund for a walk each day; it helps keep him trim and is good for his mental health (and, no doubt, yours).

Here are some famous dachshunds:

Bertie – The writer, Pelham Grenville Wodehouse (also known as 'P. G. Wodehouse'), and his dachshund,

'Bertie', were inseparable. It seems that Bertie's sage-like demeanour was the inspiration for Wodehouse's most famous fictional character, 'Jeeves'. Jeeves was a manservant to Bertie Wooster, an upper class Englishman. Bertie constantly relied on Jeeves to get him out of his many predicaments. Other famous writers who apparently kept dachshunds were James Joyce, J. D. Salinger, William Faulkner and Danielle Steele. A search on the internet shows that people in the acting and music industry like Marlon Brando, Clark Gable, Errol Flynn, Carol Lombard, John Wayne and Madonna all had dachshunds as pets.

Napoleon – Napoleon Bonaparte loved dachshunds and kept them all his life. When he was sent into exile, one of the last dachshunds he owned was one he named after himself. Napoleon, the dog, was very well known for his bravery. Unwilling to stand down in battle, this dachshund seemed quite oblivious to his small stature. One school of thought believes that the concept of 'Napoleon Complex' originates from the dog – when someone suffers from such a complex, he is said to be a short man with too much to prove. Others believe the said concept refers to Napoleon, the man. When Napoleon, the man, died, he left clear instructions that his surviving dachshunds should be entombed with him when they died. They were.

Waldi – Waldi was the first official Olympic mascot and was created for the 1972 Summer Olympics in Munich. He represented the attributes required for athletes in the Olympics – resistance, tenacity and agility. As a mascot, the picture of Waldi's head and tail were blue while the rest of his body was divided into the various colours of the Olympic Games.

Then, there was Ladoo.

Chapter 2: I Was Chosen

It was a Wednesday afternoon in February 2004. I'd self-published my novel, The Banana Leaf Men, approximately six months before. My joy was short lived because a stranger trashed my novel and launched a series of hurtful personal attacks on the internet. I went into a downward spiral of depression and despair. The sadness was unbearable and the silence in my flat was deafening. Then, like the proverbial light bulb coming on, I knew what would make me happy. Some people buy a dream car; others invest in a dream home or go on a dream holiday. I decided to get my dream dog.

By 5 p.m., I drove to the pet shop in the next suburb. Why the pet shop? Well, I'd given up on asking the animal shelter for a dachshund – when I made enquiries, the staff at the animal shelter weren't willing to talk to me because I live in a flat; I was also told that all flat dwellers are terrible people who get dogs, then abandon them. I didn't know any breeders at the time and I was desperate to get the dog right away. Any delay, even by a day, would give me time to reflect and I didn't want to change my mind.

Well before I began to look for a dog, I already knew its name: male or female, my dog would be called Ladoo. I first heard it from my friend, Harbhans Singh, whose daughter had given this name to one of her dogs. It is the name of an Indian dessert.

So, I got into my car and began driving around Brickfields. I had a vague idea that there was a pet shop somewhere around. My initial excitement was soon tinged with anxiety.

Am I doing the right thing? Should I get a dog? How will I look after it? Will it bite others? What will people think?

My mother was going to be furious I was taking on another responsibility. After all, I'd been out of a job for just over a year.

Would the management really cause a fuss?

Residents weren't supposed to keep dogs. It is ironic, but there would have been no objection if I had chosen to keep cats, fish, turtles, monitor lizards or even snakes. Dogs, however, were (and still are) not allowed.

I spotted the pet shop and parked my car nearby. On the pavement, there was a cage with a puppy inside. It did not even lift its head when I walked over to say hello. A shop assistant noticed me trying to coax this non-responsive puppy and invited me inside.

The shop's walls were lined with cages and there were puppies in all of them. None of them looked like long-bodied dachshunds to me. Sensing my growing despair, the assistant offered to help. When I told her what I wanted, she pointed to a cage behind me. I turned around, saw three black puppies and frowned. Again, none of these puppies had a long body. Had it not been for the tag with a bold print displaying their breed, I would not have guessed they were dachshunds.

The assistant informed me that these puppies (two female and one male) were for sale. I told her I was interested in the male puppy and wanted to know how much he cost. She told me to wait and went further inside the shop. I could hear her speaking to someone. I followed her. Behind the screen that separated this 'office' from the rest of the store, a stout man was seated behind a table pulling at three strands of thick hair growing from the mole on his chin. When he saw me, he stopped talking. I guessed he was the owner of the pet shop.

I swallowed and said, "I want the male dog. The dachshund. How much?"

The Boss (as I decided to call him), turned his head to one side and looked at me from the corner of his eye. "I give you discount. RM800.00."

"Hah? Why so expensive?"

"Cheap-lah. I already give discount."

I frowned. "I will buy today. You give some more discount-lah."

The Boss reached for his giant, A4-sized calculator and punched some numbers into the machine. "OK-lah. OK-lah. I give you. Which dog you want? RM750.00."

I smiled. "I want the male dog."

The Boss looked up at me. "You live in flat or house?"

"Flat. Why?"

"You can keep dog or not?"

Not him as well.

The Boss must have guessed I was not going to answer because he said, "Better if you get a female dog."

"Why-ah? More difficult with female dog, isn't it?"

The Boss shook his head from side to side. "No. You think first. Female dogs just go down. With male dog, all your walls will be stained." When he saw that I was still confused, he added, "With pee-pee."

I exhaled and looked away. He had a point. I didn't fancy having to clean my walls every time the dog urinated. It would be much easier to train the dog to go in the balcony and wash it after that.

Then, there was that other dilemma. It was a little embarrassing to have to ask him, but there was no one else I could think of who could provide an immediate and suitable answer. So, I lowered my voice, leaned towards him and asked, "Now you make me buy a female dog, I must know when it can have puppies."

"You will know one. No problem. When your dog is in heat, then you bring here and I'll send to the male dog. Can have more puppies and I sell for you. Can make money."

I waved my hand. "No. No. I don't want to breed her," I insisted. "I just want to know when she can have puppies. So, when will she be in heat?"

I felt his hesitation before he replied softly, "Maybe one year."

I carried on. "How will I know she's in heat?" I asked.

The Boss's cheeks became red. "The dog will get its period."

"But, how-ah? How will I know she's having her period?"

With barely concealed exasperation, he replied, "You'll see blood everywhere."

"Oh …" I pursed my lips and nodded. Makes sense, I suppose. Nevertheless, could I cope with this problem of a female dog being in heat, what with all that anxiety and tension? I had a choice: stains on the wall or blood everywhere. Perhaps, a female dog would be better.

But which one to choose? Both the female puppies had silky black coats with distinct markings; both were active and seemed healthy. As I mulled over this new problem, I received a phone call from a former colleague, Rajasingam. When I told him where I was and my current dilemma, he gave me this piece of advice: "You wait until the shop closes. Then, ask the owner to let all three puppies out. See which one comes to you. That will be your dog. You never choose a dog, it chooses you."

After the phone call ended, I explained what I needed to The Boss and paid him the deposit. How his demeanour changed when he saw the money! He looked around the shop and said, "O.K.-lah, I close shop early for you. Already 6.45 also."

I sat down on a plastic stool and watched as the assistant let the two female puppies out of the cage. They spent five minutes exploring every part of the shop. Then, slowly, one made her way gingerly to me and licked my toes. She looked up, climbed onto my knees and looked deeply into my eyes. We fell in love. This was my Ladoo. For an infinitesimal moment, I was tempted to take the other puppy as well. The thought of how much my mother was going to scold me was the main deterrent. I picked Ladoo up and told The Boss to put the other puppy back in the cage.

The Boss and his assistant then used a gadget to scan Ladoo's neck and showed me that a microchip had been embedded in her neck. They gave me her identification number and told me to collect her the next day as they wanted to bathe her.

Ladoo in her first bed

Once home, I moved the furniture around to make space for the little one. I had two places for her to sleep – the balcony and a corner in the sitting room (in case she felt cold at night). I set up a new feeding station in the kitchen, found some old towels and, by midnight, they were washed and drying on the clothesline in the balcony.

I didn't sleep much that night. I was excited at being able to fulfil my dream of having a dachshund. At the same time, I was petrified about how to tell my parents that I had bought a dog. Still, when the time came to Ladoo the next day, I didn't hesitate one bit. I knew I couldn't let Ladoo down; after all, I was chosen.

Chapter 3: An Indian Dog

Race and religion are often used to define every aspect of one's life, including Ladoo's. It might seem illogical to make the link between dog and race, but please bear with me.

From the Boss, I already knew that dachshunds were not the dog of choice amongst his clients. Instead, Shih Tzus, Jack Russell terriers, Alsatians and Rottweilers were far more popular. I was not surprised. After all, a long time ago, someone once said to me, "Dachshunds are ugly dogs. That long body makes them so disproportionate." I didn't have the courage to stand up for dachshunds, then. Now, I ignore such comments. I've also learned to find beauty in dogs that are perceived as ugly. For instance, the many wrinkles in English Bulldogs make me think that they are very wise animals. The overbite in Pekingese gives me reason to wonder if an orthodontist could make a living from treating dogs. Dobermans look so cute when they wag their stump of a tail. What can I say about Basset Hounds? My heart just melts looking into those soulful eyes.

Over the years, I've come to accept, albeit grudgingly, that not everyone will love Ladoo as whole-heartedly as I do. Still, I did not see what was coming one afternoon in July 2006. That day, I was on the telephone when someone rang my doorbell. I put the caller on hold and answered the door. It was my neighbour (I still don't know her name and have decided to call her Almira after the wicked witch in the wizard of Oz). She shouted at me, then stormed off. Stunned, I closed my door, ended the phone call and went outside to speak with her.

When I rang her doorbell, she answered the door, but kept the grille between us locked, thereby, making it obvious that I was not to enter her flat.

"What is wrong? Why are you so angry?"

Almira hesitated before saying, "Your dog barks."

I frowned at her, tempted to ask, "What did you expect it to do? Talk to you in English?"

Almira responded to my silence with, "You must take your dog to a specialist."

I waited a while before asking, "Why are you so angry with my dog? You are always complaining that security is bad. With this dog, there is more security."

"I don't care. Your dog has problems. You have to take it to the specialist."

I still couldn't understand why she insisted I take Ladoo to the vet. "What do you mean?"

"You take to the doctor. He can … you know, cut." She lifted her chin and pointed to her throat.

I inhaled deeply. "Are you telling me to have my dog's vocal cords cut?"

She shrugged before saying, with growing confidence, "Many people do it, what?"

I didn't say a word. Instead, I listened as she complained further about how Ladoo barked at her guests every time they walk past my closed front door to enter her flat. She had been keeping all this anger to herself for so long. Ladoo is the most badly behaved dog she has come across. She had informed the management that my dog should be shot.

I lifted my head to look at Almira. "You went to management?"

Realising that she had said too much, she took a step back and said, "I'm warning you Aneeta." She wagged her stubby finger at me and shut the door in my face.

I went immediately to the management office and asked to speak to the manager. I was instructed to go to the other side of a partition that separates the manager's office from the reception area. A lady, who seemed harassed by the fact she had to work at all, invited me to sit down. She introduced herself as the manager and, with an air of arrogance, confirmed that a complaint had been made against my dog. The management would be taking action. She recited the provision in the by-laws which prohibit residents from keeping pets in the house. I listened for a while longer before I lost my temper.

"Your by-laws say people cannot keep pets, yes? The word is 'pets', yes?"

She nodded, startled by my harsh tone.

"I swear, if you take action against me, I will go knocking on every single flat in this property and tell them that they have to get rid of all their pets. This includes every single cat, fish, bird, cicak and biawak. And I will say that this is because of you and that neighbour of mine."

"Sabar, Cik Aneeta. Sabar."

I put my hand up to stop her talking. "I'm telling you. If you touch my licensed dog, I'll sue you, I'll sue the management and I will sue that stupid neighbour." And I walked out.

I spent the rest of the day pacing in my flat. I wondered if my neighbour was capable of enticing Ladoo to the front door, prising it open and, thereafter, harming my baby. I talked the matter over with my parents and friends. We came up with a plan, which didn't seem to make sense at the time, but would do the trick of keeping Ladoo away from the door.

The next morning, I went to Carrefour and bought a child safety gate and planned how and when I was going to install it. For one, I knew that if I did not make a big hue and cry about installing this child safety gate, Almira would give me even more trouble. I also knew that she left her flat every afternoon at about 2.30 p.m. to pick up her children.

Armed with this knowledge, I asked the management if they would allow one of their staff members to help me install this gate. The staff member arrived at about 2.15 p.m. Throughout the 45 minutes it took for him to install the child safety gate, Ladoo did not bark at all. She only barked when Almira walked past.

Ladoo behind bars

Once the task was over and the staff member left, I prepared a three-page letter to the management setting out everything that had happened and all the actions I'd taken thus far. I also pointed out that when I took Ladoo for a walk, other residents, cleaners and the guards were very happy to see her. The dog was friendly and greeted them joyously. At no time had she ever harmed any of them. My aim was to make a contemporaneous record of events.

True enough, my neighbour caused more trouble. Five days later, I received a formal notice of the complaint from the management. I went to the office to give them my letter. The manager sympathised with me and told me she was only doing her job. She was used to this lady complaining all the time and asked me to forgive her. Tongue-in-cheek, the manager attempted humour by saying that my neighbour was probably going through menopause. I stared at the manager, then left without a word.

When the door to the lift opened on my floor and I stepped out, I could see my neighbour cooking in her outdoor kitchen which faces the corridor. Unable to resist a confrontation, I stood outside my flat, turned to her and said, "I want to talk to you."

Almira pretended to ignore me. I called out to her again. Above the hiss of water being added to a hot wok, she responded with, "What you want? I very bee-see one, you know."

I lifted my left eyebrow. "You're not busy enough to complain to the management. Why did you do it? You saw me putting that barrier so that my dog doesn't come near the door."

Almira placed a plate next to the stove and dumped all the contents of the wok on it. Some of what looked like black bean sauce splashed on her housecoat. Picking up a cloth from the sink, she raised her voice and said, "You cannot keep dogs, you know. DBKL (City Hall) says so."

"The dog is not going to come near you. So, what do you want now?"

Still rubbing the black bean sauce off her clothes, she insisted, "I don't care. You're not supposed to keep dogs."

I waited a moment, then changed tactics. "Why are you so bothered about my dog? There is another dog on the other side of this corridor. It barks more than my dog. Why are you complaining about my dog?"

Almira threw the cloth into the sink and looked directly at me. Pointing in the direction of the other flat, she said, "That dog is O.K. That dog is Chinese."

I stared at her for quite a while. Then, I turned away went into my flat. I sat on the sofa and, soon, Ladoo was at my feet and I saw the confusion on her face – she could not understand why I was laughing so hard. How could I explain to her that my neighbour's hatred for her was because, in Almira's eyes, Ladoo is an Indian dog?

Chapter 4: Ladoo and Her Ten Names

Ladoo has not one or two, but ten names and here's how she acquired them.

Ladoo
Many people have told me, and I agree, that I made a mistake as 'Ladoo' is the wrong way to spell my dog's name. In my defence, I was not thinking straight when the clerk at the vet's office first asked to spell her name.

This is how it all happened: It was March 2004 and I was taking Ladoo for her first visit to the vet. When I reached the clinic, the clerk told me to place the puppy inside a cage to prevent Ladoo from running all over the place.

The moment I put Ladoo inside the cage, she started to panic and began to cry. Although I tried to tell her to be quiet, she behaved as though I had abandoned her. It was altogether most disconcerting as I couldn't concentrate fully on the clerk's words.

Somewhere in the cacophony she caused, I gathered that the clerk's name was also Anita. She asked for my details and offered to fill out a patient card for me. Then, she looked at me and asked, in Malay, "Dog's name?"

"Ladoo," I said, proud I'd chosen such a unique name.

The blank look on her face was the first indication that she did not share my enthusiasm. She said, "Ha?"

"Ladoo," I repeated, but in a less confident tone this time.

"Spell," she said and held the pen, poised to write what I said.

Spell it? I blinked. Didn't everyone know how to spell ladoo?

I never once thought about how to spell it. I gathered my thoughts, licked my lips and said, "Errr … l, a, d, o, o."

"L, what?" she asked and I repeated the spelling.

Once I saw 'Ladoo' printed on the card, though, I realised my mistake. It didn't look or feel right. In hindsight, I should have insisted that the spelling be corrected to 'Laddoo'. Still, all these years have passed and everyone's just become used to 'Ladoo'.

It's rather embarrassing when the vet tells me he knows when we're visiting as Ladoo's the only one of his patients who wails this much.

Winsgurads Norris
About a month or so after Ladoo arrived, I went back to the pet shop to retrieve a certificate confirming Ladoo's pedigree. This document, issued by the Malaysian Kennel Association, uses words like 'Dam' to refer to the mother of the dog and 'Sire' for the father.

Looking through Ladoo's family tree, I laughed at some of the names of her ancestors and how she was 'made'. Ladoo's mother was, 'Winsguards Silver' and her father, 'Wenghengken Abraham'. Her paternal grandfather was 'Grandshirevale Open Minded'.

And, here's the scandalous and rather incestuous part of this story: Ladoo's grandfather ('Grandshirevale Open Minded') is also her great-grandfather.

The other interesting names of her ancestors are 'FoongFattKen Max Factor,' 'Limela Candy', 'Yenkenn Felix', 'Foonfattken Maxie Sophie', 'Harilela's Chanee', 'Chamberlain Bonfinnie' and 'GreenWarrior Dorothy'.

And what of Ladoo's actual name? Since I chose to have Ladoo spayed, I never bothered to comply with the requirements of the Malaysian Kennel Association to officially change Ladoo's name. So, my four-legged baby was officially 'Winsguards Norris' throughout her life.

"Mummy, do I look sexy in this baju?"

Laju

Each morning, at around 6 a.m., I took Ladoo for a walk. Over the years, she and I made friends with the many people who also went for a walk then. For instance, there was a lady from the 15th floor who took her children to school each day and never failed to say hello. There was a furry little doggie, Toto, who kissed Ladoo each time they met (much to Ladoo's disdain, I should add). One lady spent her time waiting for her daughter to arrive by going down on her knees and playing with Ladoo.

Then, there was what happened with one of our Indonesian guards:

"What name your dog?" He put his hand out for my ever-eager dog to sniff.

"Ladoo," I replied, holding on to her leash that much tighter, afraid that this guard's enthusiasm for the dog was just momentary. Besides, the smell of the Gudang Garam cigarette-cum-cheroot he was smoking this early in the morning was too much; I wanted to get away fast.

"Oh. Laju." He snuffed out his cigarette-cum-cheroot and squatted in front of the dog.

"No. Not, Laju. Ladoo." I held the leash even tighter.

"R? Like Raju?"

"No. L-"

Before I could finish spelling her name, he interjected with, "Oh, L. Like speed."

Speed? I frowned. Then it dawned on me. Laju. 'Laju' is Malay for speed.

"Laju," he called out.

Ladoo wagged her tail and I tried once again. "No. La-doo." I said the word slowly and deliberately, hoping he'd understand what I was saying.

He looked up at me and nodded purposefully.

Great! He's got it.

He petted Ladoo and said, "Hello Laju."

I gave up.

Ladoo Dog
There were times when I was certain that Ladoo didn't think she was a dog, like the times she stood in front of a mirror and examined her reflection. She'd look up at me and back at her reflection and frown, as though asking, "How come, you look so different?" To make sure that we both knew and, more importantly, accepted, that she's a dog and of a different species, I sometimes called her, "Ladoo Dog".

Fatso and Manja
I was constantly reminded that my dog, being a dachshund, had that long body and was, therefore, prone to having spinal problems. I was instructed to watch her weight all the time. But when her stomach was full, I couldn't resist watching her waddle towards me when I called out, "Come here, Fatso."

Sometimes, she'd go all round the flat in search of me. When she found me, she'd rush to demand affection. How could I resist the opportunity to give her tummy a rub? The cuddling after that, of course, led to name calling on my part ("Manja") and lots of sighing from Ladoo.

Lads and Dog
"Lads" and "Dog" were for those days when, "Ladoo" was just too long and tedious to say.

Long Dog
"Long Dog" was, naturally, for the times I referred to Ladoo's long body.

Ladoo Bladoo
"Ladoo Bladoo" is for days when I felt creative and poetic. After all, "Ladoo Bladoo" did rhyme quite nicely.

Ladoo Sundararaj and Bad Dog
I've heard that many mothers call out their child's full name when the child misbehaves. Similarly, when Ladoo did something wrong, I'd shout, "Ladoo Sundararaj." If she'd done something particularly bad, then I'd follow this with, "Bad Dog". She'd stand very still and lower her head. Gingerly looking up at me, she would gauge my reaction and showed me the tip of her tongue, as though to say, "Sorry." Most times, I'd give in at this point and forgive her. However, on the few occasions when her misdemeanour was particularly bad (like the time she dismantled a bed spread I was making), I made her sit in one spot for a good 15 minutes and intermittently said, "Bad Dog".

Ladoo, I love you
I kept this name for when Ladoo was moody and grumpy. I usually started with "Ladoo". When she still refused to come to me, I'd lower my voice and say tenderly, "Ladoo, I love you." Without hesitation, she always came running to me.

With so many names, it wasn't surprising that when I did call her just "Ladoo," she often frowned, thoroughly confused.

Chapter 5: Stretch Dog

When people hear that my dog's name was Ladoo, they often ask me, "If you had another dog, what name will you give it?" Well, here's a list of names that have fascinated me and the stories that come with them.

Jilebi
Many Indians assume that I'll name another dog Jilebi as ladoos often go with jilebis. What are jilebis? They're another favourite North Indian sweetmeat. It's always such a pleasure to bite into one and taste the sweet syrup oozing out of a jilebi.

Still, can you imagine what it'll be like having to call out "Jilebi" each time? Three-syllabled names are hard to shout out. Worse, they could be shortened to form something that sounds quite unsavoury, like what happened to my friend. She loved the name 'Gitanjali' and was determined to give that name to her child. When her daughter was born, my friend consulted an astrologer to find out what letter the baby's name should start with. She also consulted a numerologist to see the appropriate 'number' that the name should add up to. Combine stars, numbers and determination and the child ended up being called 'Kheetanjelly'; naturally, her pet name is 'Jelly'.

Patisa
Again, this is the name of a sweet. While Patisa sounds nice, it's a little difficult to call out, "Patisa." It would be shortened to "Patis" and that doesn't sound at all endearing.

Karma

Karma has become quite a fashionable term and an online dictionary explains that 'karma is the cosmic principle of rewarding or punishing a person in one incarnation according to that person's deeds in the previous incarnation; karma is fate or destiny; karma is the good or bad emanations felt to be generated by someone or something.' Frankly, as interesting and fascinating as the name is, I think I'll suffer from an attack of conscience each time I called out to my dog if I named it Karma.

Hanuman

Hanuman is one of those characters in Hindu mythology that always has an element of witticism about him. He is also affectionately referred to as 'the monkey god'. He is the only character present in both the Hindu epics of Mahabharat and Ramayana. In the Mahabharat, Hanuman positioned himself as an emblem on Arjuna's flag atop his chariot. In the Ramayana, Hanuman played a more obvious role – he flew across the ocean to Lanka and located Sita, Ram's wife, who was being held in captivity. With such an important role that Hanuman played in Hindu mythology, I always wanted to name my dog Hanuman. This is what happened when I told my mother.

"I think I'll name my next dog Hanuman."

My mother's face lost its softness. "I think it's terrible to name your dog Hanuman."

I frowned. "But why?"

My mother cut up her toast with more force than was necessary. "It's a god's name. It's so disrespectful."

"But can you see how much I'll love this dog? I think the gods will be so pleased with the affection I show one of their creatures."

"No." There's a tone of finality in this response. I knew better than to argue with her.

Over the years, every time I even mention the name Hanuman, my mother cringes and I've been made to promise that I'll never name any dog of mine Hanuman.

Sanyasin
A sanyasin is a renunciant who gives up all ties to the material world and dedicates his life to God. Some of the most famous renunciants are Adi Shankaracharya and Paramahansa Yogananda. The former was an Indian philosopher who consolidated the doctrine of Advaita (non-duality). The latter wrote a classic book, 'Autobiography of a Yogi'. Anyway, when I told a friend that I liked the name Sanyasin, he promptly told me that I would plant the idea of celibacy into my dog's head and probably make him impotent. That was the end of Sanyasin.

Bhima

Our family friends used to have two Great Danes. They were named Bhiman and Bindu. In the Mahabharat, Bhima is one of the five Pandava brothers. He is strong, mighty and fearless. He is also the Hanuman's half-brother – they share the same father, Vayu (the lord of the winds).

Our friend's house has a very wide doorway and the dogs were never allowed inside. After all, one swish of Bhiman's tail and there was bound to be very little furniture left. Still, these huge dogs had the gentlest nature and the most soulful eyes I've ever seen. They sat outside, but placed their chin just inside the threshold, looking at us longingly, apologetically and sorrowfully, as if to say, "I know I can't come in. I'm too big." One day, their master returned from work to find the dogs missing. Bhiman and Bindu were dog-napped and never found. I'd like to think that they went to a family that loved them. Alas, I suspect they were made into soup.

Gorby
My aunt had a lovely Alsatian, Gorby, named after Gorbachev. By the time I met him, he was old, but he loved the attention I gave him – I took him one of those knotted bones made from natural beef hide. I made the mistake of taking one that was too large and this dog didn't quite know how to eat it. Still, he never let go of it and carried it around with him like a prized toy.

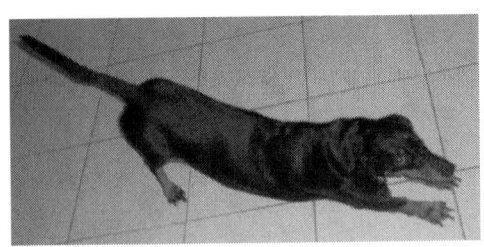

Ladoo demonstrating the 'Downward Dog' technique for those who practice yoga.

Stretch

When there are stretch limos, doesn't it make perfect sense that dachshunds are stretch dogs? The name 'Stretch' also reminds me of yoga. Anyone who practises yoga will be familiar with the term 'Downward Dog' or 'Adho Mukha Svanasana'. Some of the instructions are "Spread your fingers" and "Keep your seat bone up". I didn't quite understand what these meant until I observed Ladoo when she stretched.

All said and done, even though I have thought of all sorts of names, I have no idea what name I'll give any other dog that comes into my life. We'll just have to wait and see.

Chapter 6: Grandpa's Darling

I hear stories of people who are stern parents. However, when the same people become grandparents, it's completely different: they spoil their grandchildren to the point of frustrating the parents. It appears to be the same with my father and Ladoo. I was always aware that my father was fond of dogs, but I never knew how much until Ladoo came into our lives.

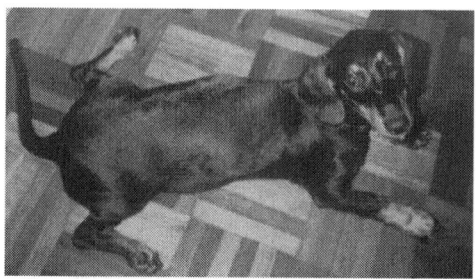

"You called, Mummy?"

Here are three incidents that showcase how much Ladoo was Grandpa's darling. And, yes, as my father has finally admitted, we're related to Ladoo – I'm 'Mummy' and my father is 'Grandpa'.

Look at me, Grandpa. I'm free!
It was the time of Ladoo's third visit to my parents' home. My mother had gone overseas and Ladoo and I were keeping my father company. Ladoo must have been no more than ten months old and was still mischievous and naughty. Each morning, I'd wake up, come downstairs, play with her, read the papers, let her out into the garden and go upstairs to have a shower. The

tinkling of her bell let us know that she was fine and happy in the garden.

One day, after my shower, I came downstairs and my father was sitting at the dining table. He had shaving cream on half his face and was holding a razor in one hand. He was sweating and wheezing slightly.

"What's wrong?" I was alarmed.

My father looked at me and said with difficulty, "Wait. Palpitations."

My father cannot have palpitations. He's a heart patient. Any stress to his heart and it's a worry for us all. "Why? What happened?"

He struggled to say, "Give me water, first."

When I entered the kitchen, I saw Ladoo sitting in one corner. She refused to make eye contact. I poured my father a glass of water and took it to him. He drank the water in one go. Then he put the glass down on the table and told me the story. While he was shaving, he suddenly realised that all was quiet in the garden. He called out to Ladoo, expecting to hear the sound of a tinkling bell. However, there was only silence. He began to panic. With razor in one hand, he went to the front door, opened it and called out her name. Still, there was no reply. Then, he heard the faint tinkle of that bell.

"I had such a fright."

"Why?" Surely there was nothing wrong. Ladoo couldn't have got lost in the garden.

"She wasn't inside the garden. She was outside the gate. I had to open the gate and shout at her to come in." He put his hand on his chest to steady his heartbeat.

My jaw dropped. "But, how did she get out?"

"I don't know," my father replied. "There must be a hole in the fence somewhere. Someone could have taken her away." He kept shaking his head in disbelief. I knew that he, too, was thinking of what might have happened had Ladoo been dog-napped like our friend's Great Danes, Bhiman and Bindu.

"Never mind. She's O.K. now," I said, hoping my father would calm down.

"Yes. But anything could have happened to her. She's a special dog."

I hid my smile. Special dog, indeed.

I walked over to where Ladoo was. She would not look at me. Indeed, she didn't make eye-contact with anyone in the house for the rest of the day.

Thereafter, Ladoo was not allowed into the garden on her own. An adult had to accompany her when she needed to go outside. My father also made a thorough inspection of the garden in search of the offending hole in the fence. We never found it, but, by the time Ladoo visited again, my father called a contractor and had his whole fence re-done. The contractor made sure that all gaps were plugged and the drains properly cemented. My father was satisfied that his four-legged grandchild would never again escape.

Grandpa, save me
When I was in school, each year, the girls gave the principal a parting gift. One year, the girls' gift was a white Labrador puppy called Molly. I met Molly twice in her lifetime and she was lovely. My enduring memory of her is that she loved going to the beach and nothing gave her more joy than to run into the water and chase the waves.

Sadly, I can't say the same about Ladoo because she hated water. If there was a puddle of water on the road, unlike other dogs who make it point to get their feet wet, Ladoo walked around it.

Ladoo's bath began with me spreading a towel on the floor outside the bathroom. Then, I removed her collar and coaxed Ladoo into the bathroom. If a hole could open up in the floor at that moment, I think Ladoo would gladly sink into the hole. She curled her body into a little ball. No amount of cajoling, even with food, succeeded. Most times, I ended up carrying her into the bathroom. After her bath, though, it was a different story altogether. She no longer wore that martyred look. She was frisky and behaved as though she'd done us all a favour by having a bath.

One day, when I was in Alor Star, I took her collar off in the kitchen and went in search of her shampoo. When I went to collect her, she was nowhere to be found. Instead, she'd gone to her one 'saviour' – my father.

He was busy polishing all his shoes and I could see Ladoo sitting on one of them. With a shoe in one hand and the brush in another, he looked up at me and frowned.

"Ladoo, come here," I said.

"Grandpa, please save me. Grandpa? Please? I love you, Grandpa!"

She inched her bottom closer to my father, but still refused to look at me. Then, she tilted her head to one side and looked at him, her eyes huge with a desperate plea in them. If she could talk, I think these are the words she would have used to beg him: "Please Grandpa, save me. Pul-eese Grandpa. I love you, Grandpa. I'm a good girl."

My father was still confused. "Look here, what is your dog doing?"

I sighed and said, "She's seeking your protection."

"Huh?"

"I have to give her a bath. So, she's asking if you'll protect her from me."

My father dropped the shoe and brush immediately. He bent forward to pat Ladoo. Tenderly, he said, "It's O.K. It's only a bath. Go, Ladoo, go. Go to Mummy."

My heart melted.

Nonetheless, Ladoo was not persuaded and refused to budge. In the end, I had no choice, but to pick her up and take her for her bath.

Grandpa, my friend
Tea time is special in my parents' house. It's a time when all of us get together and eat too much. At any given time, there are biscuits, nuts, cakes and kuih-kuih. Then, on special days, there can be upama, curry-puffs or even a char koay teow. Ladoo has learnt to sit by my father's side as he drops bits of food to her.

One afternoon, while my father was having a nap, I went out to buy some layer cake for tea. When I came home, Ladoo was, as always, overjoyed to see me. She was even happier that I had food in my hands.

I was in the kitchen, cutting this layer cake into several pieces when, suddenly, I heard my father screaming. I dropped everything and ran to his room.

There he was, lying very near the edge of the bed, wiping his lips with the back of his hand. Ladoo was dancing nearby.

"What happened? Are you O.K?"

"No-lah," my father replied. Wiping his mouth with the back of his hand, he said, "It's your dog. It's terrible. She licked my lips and kissed me."

I burst out laughing. Apparently, Ladoo had barked several times, but my father ignored her and continued to sleep. Frustrated and desperate to get his attention, she licked his lips. Not his cheek or forehead. Instead, she went straight for his lips.

I think the kiss was Ladoo's way of saying, "Wake up, Grandpa. It's tea time and Mummy's brought something new. Feed me, Grandpa. Feed me."

Needless to say, my father does not sleep so close to the edge of the bed anymore.

Chapter 7: Ladoo Upstairs

On 3rd of November 2010, I drove from Alor Star to Penang for a lunch appointment. As I made my way to the highway, I could see the water levels of the Sungai Muda river rising. I didn't think much of this. After all, the same thing happened in 2007 when it rained non-stop and our garden was flooded. When I returned from Penang in the evening, however, the water level had risen far too much.

The next day, our electricity supply was cut off. Soon, there was no water either. I became distressed, especially when our friends telephoned to say that they were leaving Alor Star and going to stay with their children in Penang. I remember the panic in my mother's voice when she heard that the prediction was that the water levels would rise to ten feet. When the phone call ended, there was a heated debate in our house. Should we go? Or, should we stay? Finally, my father made his decision: he refused to leave his house. I refused to leave my parents. So, Ladoo and I would have to stay.

All afternoon, I watched our neighbours, one by one, leave their houses and wondered if we'd made the right choice. The water kept rising and, by tea time, we could no longer open our gate. I spotted our resident iguana swimming in the garden. No way was Ladoo going out, even if it meant having to clean up after her inside the house.

We prepared for dinner early. It was also the eve of Deepavali and we had to say prayers for my departed grandparents. After dinner, which was rather sumptuous (rice, mutton curry, chicken curry, beans and Indian sweetmeats) considering our predicament, there was nothing to do but go to sleep.

At about 3 a.m. I woke up. I could hear some noise downstairs. Using the torch-light, I went to investigate downstairs. Our maid said that water had already entered the house. I followed her and, true enough, there was water rising in our storeroom and the bathroom. When I opened the front door, if the water level rose by even an inch, we would have had water in the sitting room as well.

When she came downstairs, the maid suggested we evacuate the house and she would stay. I stared at her. If anything happened to her, how would we face her family? Imagine having to say to her children, "I'm sorry. The water was rising. We made our escape, but left your mother to look after the house." Her warped logic was that she could better manage the flood without having us to worry about. While I appreciated the concern our maid had for us, there was no way we were leaving her behind. Besides, my mother made a pertinent point: even if we got out of the house, there was no guarantee that the car would not get stuck in the middle of the road. It would be wiser to stay put. So, at 3 a.m., we decided to transfer food and necessities upstairs in case the water rose too much. This included making a place for Ladoo.

For the next three hours, we took all things that we considered precious upstairs. This included the laptop, family photographs and some of my grandfather's artefacts. Throughout, Ladoo followed me around, but whimpered whenever I went upstairs.

In hindsight, we also did some silly things. For instance, I remember taking all the cushions from the sofa upstairs. But we never took the sofa proper because it was too heavy. If the sofa got washed away, of what use were the cushions that we'd saved?

"Which way, Mummy? Don't be scared. I'll drive you to safety."

On normal days, Ladoo's carpet is placed in a very strategic place in the house – it's at the foot of the stairs and near the dining room. From this spot, she can see what's happening in the kitchen and who is at the gate. She can also keep an eye on my father in his room and watch who goes up and down the stairs. She's never allowed to come upstairs. That day, at 6 a.m., was the one and only time Ladoo was carried upstairs and slept on her mat outside my room.

Ladoo used this opportunity to investigate every corner of my room, the guest room and the bathroom. She avoided my parents' bedroom. It was as if she knew my mother would never approve. Even in my flat, when we're alone, Ladoo moves about freely. But when my mother visits, Ladoo never steps inside the room my mother occupies. Nothing is cuter than watching a dachshund stand at the doorway of a bedroom and stretch her long body to observe what's happening inside.

"My side profile's better."

The next evening, having spent the day with no internet, phone or radio, I had nothing to do but to observe the situation and circumstances we found ourselves in. It became clear to me that the water was being let out in stages. My theory was that the whole process was timed to coincide with low tide – whenever I heard the helicopter overhead, I knew the water would rise again within the hour. For instance, when we heard the helicopter at 10 p.m., the water level would start to rise by midnight and be at its highest at about 3 a.m. Then, it would recede by 6 a.m. In time, this knowledge became extremely useful as I used the periods when the water receded to encourage Ladoo to go outside and ease herself.

No one really knows why these floods happened. Some blamed the excessive rain and others blamed poor management. The rumour was this: there was a lot of rain in southern Thailand. If the authorities did not release the water there, people would die. When water was released, some of it came into Malaysia and we were flooded. I doubt we'll ever know what really happened. The fear I have is that it might happen again.

Throughout this experience, I learnt something new: my parents are far more resilient than I am. While I panicked and fussed, both of them were sure that things would be fine. Some friends did make fun of me saying that I, being the youngest, should have been the brave one. I think this is a little unfair. After all, this was the first time in my life when we were completely cut off from the outside world. We've had no electricity supply, no water supply, and sometimes, our gate refuses to open. But, never have all of these happened at the same time.

As for my little doggie, although our connection with the outside world was severed for a mere 48 hours, it was many days after electricity and water supply were restored before she ventured into the garden alone. She wasn't going to get her feet wet unnecessarily.

Chapter 8: Ladoo and the Tsunami

In March 2011, as I watched the tsunami in Japan on TV, like many others, I prayed for the victims of this natural disaster and marvelled at how earthquake-proof many of the Japanese buildings are. In the aftermath of the disaster, I was impressed with the fortitude and discipline of the Japanese people in rebuilding their lives.

It brought back memories of the time Ladoo and I were caught in what the international scientific community has come to call, The Great Sumatra-Andaman Earthquake and its deadly twin, The Asian Tsunami of 2004.

At the time, Ladoo was just over a year old and had undergone surgery to have her spayed. The procedure was carried out on 23rd December and it went without a hitch. It would have been so much better for my mental state had she been allowed to recuperate at the vet's surgery. However, there was another dog that had some problems and Ladoo was not allowed to stay for fear of cross-infection. So, I had to bring her home and look after her. I prayed that I would do nothing wrong.

My biggest challenge was to keep her from moving around too much. It did not help that my father had engaged contractors at the time to paint the house. With all these people going in and out of the house, Ladoo was excited and wanted to chase after them all the time.

On the morning of 26th December, Ladoo was particularly fussy. She would not stay in one place and I was tired of running after her. I decided to put her on her leash and tie the leash to the sturdy leg of our dining table. While doing this, I felt the whole table move. I remember thinking that this little dog was very strong. Even in her less-than-optimal-state, she could move our heavy teak wood table.

I started playing with her. A few moments later, the painters propped ladders against the outer walls of the house. Suddenly I felt the house shake. Could the foundations of our house be so weak? Could three thin and weather-weary painters could shake the whole house?

A while later, my mother came downstairs and asked, "Did you feel the earthquake?"

I frowned. Then it dawned on me. "So, that's what it was."

When I told her what my actual thoughts were, we laughed for a while then went about our work not aware of the impending disaster.

The first inkling I had of the magnitude of this natural disaster was when my cousin from the UK rang to ask if we were fine. I replied, nonchalant, that things were fine. An hour later, a friend cancelled our appointment to meet up for tea. A little put out, I complained and she retorted with, "Switch on the television, Aneeta, and see what's happened."

When I did, the newscasters were just beginning to report on the places that had been destroyed in Sri Lanka, Acheh, India and Thailand. When I heard the newsreader mention Penang and Langkawi, I reached for the telephone, but it was hard to get through to anyone. The phone lines were busy for a long time. Finally, I got through to some of family and friends and confirmed that they were safe.

Watching the continuous stories on the news, I came to learn about what had happened. The earth is covered with several pieces of hard rock which fit together like a jigsaw puzzle. Each piece is called a 'plate' and these plates interact with each other along boundaries called, 'faults'. Oceanic plates slide under continental plates. When an oceanic plate tries to slide underneath the continental plate, the continental plate is dragged down. After being repeatedly pulled down, the continental plate can snap to its former shape. This is a large vertical movement of the earth's crust and is called a 'subduction earthquake'. It vertically displaces the water above it from its equilibrium by either elevating the sea floor or making it subside. In an attempt to regain its equilibrium, seawater is pushed to the surface. This generates a wave which can create a tsunami.

The word 'tsunami' is derived from two Japanese words: 'tsu' meaning 'harbour' and 'nami' meaning 'wave'. The reason that tsunamis are able to travel great distances is because the rate at which a tsunami loses its energy is inversely proportional to its wavelengths. As such, it loses little energy. This allows it to travel at great speed and over a long distance. As the tsunami approaches the coast, the wave is compressed and its speed is slowed down considerably because the waters become shallow. When it hits the shore, the tsunami loses its energy because it has encountered friction and turbulence from the sea bed. However, it reaches the coast with so much potential energy that it can strip beaches of sand, trees and vegetation. The tsunami can slow down to less than 80 km/hour have a wavelength that is about 20 kilometres and an oscillation that takes mere minutes. To those watching from the shore, the resulting wave appears as a rapidly rising tide or even a series of breaking waves.

The Great Sumatra-Andaman Earthquake, which measured between 9.1 and 9.3 on the Richter scale, was an example of a 'megathrust' earthquake. It generated the Asian Tsunami which was able to travel across oceans and caused waves as high as 15 meters in some places.

"Nothing exciting ever happens."

In the aftermath of this disaster, there were many stories of unimaginable loss and pain, people who went out of their way to donate food, clothing and medicines and doctors who went to the disaster zones to offer aid.

Observing the chaos from afar, I was grateful we were not adversely affected by this natural disaster. In fact, the memories of what happened to us, personally, during that time are trivial in comparison. For example, two days after the tsunami, Ladoo came and sat by my feet. Out of the blue, she barked at me. It was a single bark and in her puppy voice. It was the first time my little doggie showed her temper and frustration when we didn't share our food with her.

Also, during a telephone conversation with a friend on Christmas Eve, he said, "Actually, 2004 has been quite boring. Nothing exciting happened." If only he had waited two more days, he might not have said this.

Chapter 9: Dancing Kambing and Gambling

During the time of the Great Sumatra-Andaman Earthquake and Asian Tsunami, my father had engaged the services of contractors who were busy painting our house. Each evening, my father sat on the swing in our garden and watched them go about their tasks. One evening, Ladoo and I joined him. To prevent Ladoo from running around and barking at the painters, I tied her leash to one of the poles of our swing.

By then, it was already the end of the workday and only one painter remained. On 2 May 2011, Mary Schneider, a local newspaper columnist described her plumber in the following manner: 'His droopy eyes were set in a worn face, which sat upon a wrinkled neck that disappeared into an equally wrinkled shirt.' This description would fit this painter perfectly.

With a cigarette balanced between his teeth, the painter climbed down the ladder. By the time he put his foot down on the ground, Ladoo was almost berserk with excitement. She started to dance and go round in circles at the thought of making a new friend.

The painter stopped to admire my dog, but did not go near her. Instead, he turned to my father and spoke to my father Malay.

"See, Mummy, I told you my hands are long. I'm sure goats can't do this."

"Wah doktor, you punya kambing banyak cantik." Wah, doctor, this goat is very beautiful.

Without missing a beat, my father replied, "Apa kambing? Itu anjing, lah." What goat? That's a dog lah.

The painter looked a little closer at Ladoo and mumbled, "Oh…"

I will remember the look on his face all my life. It was a mixture of puzzlement, embarrassment and confusion. He walked away scratching his head. To give him the benefit of the doubt, I think he genuinely believed he was saying the right thing. In his mind, he meant 'dog' and thought that the Malay word for 'dog' was 'kambing'. He was baffled when my father set him right and said that Ladoo was no 'kambing', but an 'anjing'.

Something else happened during this time. You see, in Alor Star, there are no casinos (or none that I know of). What I am aware of are the mini-gambling hubs. One of them is barely 500 metres from the back of my father's house and situated opposite a wet market commonly referred to as 'Koboi Market'. Opposite this market is a row of shop houses. Most mornings, this area is full of people, but by lunchtime the market closes and the place is deserted. That said, there are a few evenings when this area becomes busy because many people come to buy their lottery tickets from companies like Kuda, Toto and Magnum.

By 2004, I figured that since I know so many people who buy these lottery tickets and often win money, I too should give it a try. This was my plan: I'd give my father enough money to invest in one number every week throughout 2005. I calculated that the amount I would have to pay for the entire year would come to about RM156.00.

So, one morning, I counted the money, put it an envelope and included a little notebook with the numbers I'd like to buy. I had it all organised and was looking for a safe place to keep it so that I could hand it to my father after breakfast.

At that moment, Ladoo started to fuss. Since she had just had her hysterectomy, I was immediately concerned for her and put the envelope down on the table to tend to her needs. When she was comfortable, I went upstairs to have a bath. I forgot all about the money I'd left on the dining table.

Long after we finished breakfast, I remembered the money. When I looked for it, it was gone. I reasoned that if Ladoo had not distracted me, I might have kept it in a safer place. I could have kicked up a big fuss and asked my father to question the contractors. But I knew that my parents were bound to scold me for being careless with money. Besides, it's so embarrassing that I lost all my money before I even started to gamble. I decided that this was a lesson from God warning me about the dangers of gambling. Now, I don't gamble at all; for this, I blame Ladoo.

Chapter 10: Sound of a Heart Breaking

I'd love to say that Ladoo had many four-legged friends; that she shares her toys with them and they love coming to play with her. Sadly, none of this is true. When she did meet other dogs, she tended to look down on them, even though she was clearly much shorter.

It's not entirely my fault. With hand on heart, I can say that I made a concerted effort to help my dog socialise with other dogs. Here's what happened.

Ladoo was five years old and she was going to be introduced to a Silky Australian terrier called Bella. My father wasn't in favour of this and warned me that it might not turn out as I hoped as Ladoo was too old. Still, I was determined to socialise my doggie.

I've known Bella since she was a puppy and this tiny thing has so much energy that Theresa once described her as the bunny in the Energizer battery advert. True enough, if you sit down, Bella won't just come up to you and hover at your feet until you play with her. She'll jump up and sit next to you to demand your attention. After she's greeted you, she doesn't jump off the chair and land on the floor. Instead, she'll jump onto the next chair and make her way round the room until she's said hello to everyone in the room.

Anyway, the play-date for the two four-legged-babies was fixed for a Saturday afternoon. The plan was to allow them to play while we adults enjoyed tea.

When Ladoo and I arrived, I rang the doorbell and Theresa opened the gate. I saw Bella at the far end of the garage. She barked her hello and that was when Ladoo started to become agitated. She barked at Bella and ran around in circles for a while.

Theresa and I took the two dogs to the porch. Imagine the scene: Theresa sat on a chair and held Bella's leash. I sat on the floor with Ladoo in my lap. Bella was straining to come and say hello to us. Only Ladoo barked in Bella's face all the time. I kept telling Ladoo, "For God's sake, she's not going to harm you. Just say hello and be nice." But Ladoo refused to listen to me and continued to bark at Bella.

I thought if Ladoo watched me saying hello to Bella first, she would see that no harm would come to her and follow suit. So, I carried Ladoo to a bench about three feet away and made her sit there. When she was calm, I walked over to Bella and started playing with her. Ladoo began to wail.

"What are you crying for? I'm here. I've not gone anywhere," I told my dog.

Ladoo wailed even more.

"If you want to know what it sounds like when a heart is breaking, just listen to your dog now," Theresa said.

Indeed, Ladoo looked as pathetic as she sounded: it was as though she'd been chained to a wall and left out in the rain for hours without food. My obsessively possessive dachshund could not bear that I'd cast her aside and had the audacity to play with another dog.

By this time, Bella's patience had reached its limit. This little doggie, about a quarter of Ladoo's size, was baring her teeth and looked quite ferocious. I can just imagine what Bella was thinking about Ladoo: 'What the hell is wrong with you? You come to my house. I welcome you, ask you to play with me. And this is how you react? Idiot!'

It was time to end this play-date. Mediating between the two four-legged-babies was not going to work. If there was to be any peace (and a cup of tea), I had to take Ladoo home. I put Ladoo's leash back on her and we walked to the front door. Theresa advised me to comfort Ladoo as "she's probably so heartbroken right now."

Feeling the pangs of guilt at putting my baby through such trauma, I kept my eyes lowered. I dreaded the scolding I was going to get from my father when I told him what had happened. But my dog was not done for the day. Before she got into the car, Ladoo fussed and I understood that she wanted to ease herself. When I took her for a walk, two houses away, a Rottweiler started to bark at us. I was a little afraid, but not Ladoo. All brave again now that she knew I had ceased to focus my attention on another dog, she looked this huge fellow straight in his face. And she barked at him. He stopped barking, stunned. I swear, if this Rottweiler could talk, it would have probably said, "What? You're barking at me? How dare you, you long, fat dog."

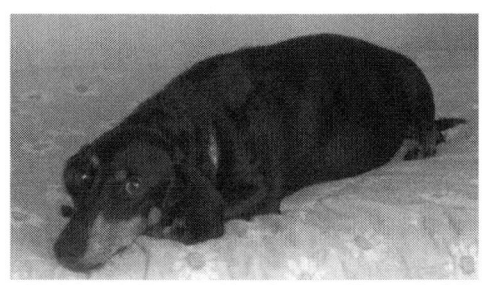

"Did that Rottweiler just call me fat?"

I didn't wait for the Rottweiler to regain his senses and come after us. I gathered my supposedly heartbroken four-legged child into my arms and left.

I did not bother to socialise Ladoo after this. Each time I thought I might attempt to find her friends of her own species, I remember how she wailed and concluded that the effort was just not worth it … for both of us.

Chapter 11: Temper Tantrum

Whenever we had visitors, in Ladoo's eyes, they'd come to see her. She was so excited that she'd go from one person to another, giving little licks. After everyone settled down, she'd look for her bone and share it with our visitors. It was her way of sharing all the love and affection in her long body with them. Most visitors were pleased and reciprocated with equal affection and petted her. There were one or two who didn't like it. But I wasn't going to bother about them because I loved this show of affection. Can you imagine how dull it would have been if you visited us and Ladoo sat in a corner, morose and depressed in the knowledge that because she's a dog, she's unwanted?

Anyway, I developed a protocol for visitors to follow: before they come into the flat, I first confined Ladoo to the bedroom. The guests came inside and we humans said hello first. Then, Ladoo came out and went berserk. Everyone had to stand still for about 30 seconds until she calmed down.

Ladoo was generally very well-behaved. When we went on our morning walks, she walked next to me and didn't bark unnecessarily. When she tried to jump on people and I told her not to, she listened. She didn't mess up the flat nor did she chew the furniture. Sometimes, when my friends were upset and came over for a shoulder to cry on, Ladoo comforted them with tenderness and warmth in a manner that I never could.

That said, underneath this lovable persona that Ladoo showed the world lay a massive temper. I didn't recognise it at first. After all, other angry dogs will probably whine, scream, fling themselves around, bare their teeth or refuse to budge. Ladoo didn't do any of these. Instead, there were several degrees to Ladoo's fury.

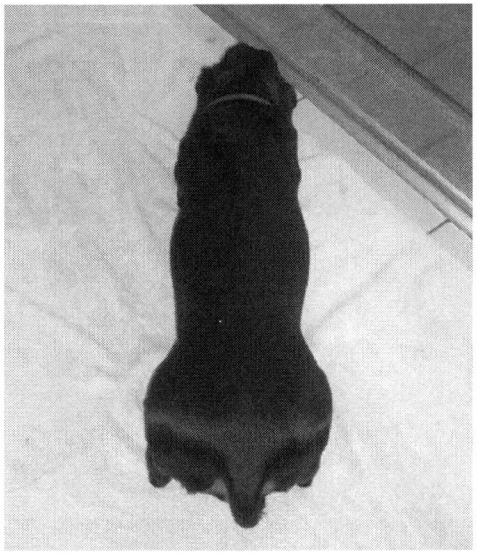

"How can Mummy scold me like that? What does she think I am? A dog?'

It started with her body being in 'prone position'. If she was facing me, I knew that she was annoyed, but would easily come round if she was allowed to do what she wanted. An example of this was when Ladoo wanted to come inside the bedroom, but wasn't allowed to. She'd sit at the threshold and look at me. Her thought process, perhaps, was this: 'I know I can't, but I'll wait; just in case Mummy decides to change her mind.'

If her back was turned to me, but her body was at an angle, Ladoo was angry, but not furious. I needed to soften the tone of my voice when I called her and she'd come running to me.

When she showed me her back, then I knew she was unhappy and angry. If her tail was tucked underneath, you could feel the absolute fury emanating from her. She was probably thinking something along the lines of 'How can Mummy do this to me? What does she think I am? A dog?'

When she chose this position, no amount of cajoling on my part helped. Ladoo had to be left alone to stew in her anger. Left alone, thought, she'd soon forget what she was angry about, become bored and fall asleep. When she gave a big sigh, I knew all was once again well in Ladoo's world.

Ladoo minding the phone.

The last time she was this furious was about two years ago. It was some time in the evening and Ladoo had just finished her dinner. I was sitting cross-legged on the floor, playing with her. My telephone rang. I rose to my feet and went to pick it up. It was my mother. This was the gist of our conversation.

"So, what are you doing?"

"Nothing. Just playing with Ladoo. Going to yoga soon." I walked to the sofa and sat down. Ladoo looked at me and then started to walk away from me. Actually, she stomped away.

"Good. Did you go to Carrefour today? Did you get those nuts I asked you to buy?"

"Yes. Wait. Hold on. I can't hear you." Ladoo was at the front door, barking at anyone who dared to walk past my flat.

I raised my voice and shouted, "Ladoo! Stop barking."

My mother said, "You see, she barks whenever when I call."

"No-lah. She barks whenever anyone calls and my attention is diverted away from her."

"How spoilt."

Quick to defend my baby, I said, "No. Not spoilt. Just loved beyond belief."

"Spoilt."

"How can you say that? She's such a darling." I turned to look for Ladoo. And I giggled.

"What's wrong?"

"Nothing. Ladoo is so angry with me. You should see her now."

I then described how Ladoo had her back to me and was clearly furious.

"You see, spoilt. You can't even talk to your own mother without her becoming jealous."

I didn't dare say this to my mother, but I often wonder who was more jealous, the dog or my mother.

Chapter 12: Friday is a Good Day

It was ten minutes past four in the evening and I was sitting on the top step of the staircase in the corridor of my block of flats. I didn't know whether my tears were because I was relieved, exhausted, sad or all of them. I couldn't cry in the flat. When a few tears did flow the night before, Ladoo, with her grossly distended abdomen, clumsily rose from her bed and waddled to sit in front of me in an attempt to comfort me. When she put her paw on my knee, I yearned to pick her up and hug her, but I couldn't because I was afraid of putting pressure on her chest which might cause her to gag.

For five months, Ladoo was unwell. The most terrifying moment was on 11th of January 2013. Ladoo hadn't been eating properly and, for anyone who knows my little one, that's bad enough. That morning, she woke me up at 5 a.m. and demanded I take her downstairs. After she evacuated her bowels, she couldn't move. When I picked her up, I saw something I'd never seen in her eyes – fear. The question was clear: "Mummy, what's happening to me? I'm scared, Mummy."

When she saw that I was equally frightened, she began to panic. Her tongue hung out, her gums became pale and she started to fade away. I hugged her close and started to pray. When we arrived home, I lay her down on a towel and used a syringe, without the needle, to force 100Plus down her throat. That gave her some energy and I repeated this regularly until we saw the vet and she was stabilised.

During the next few weeks, after blood, urine and ultrasound tests plus an X-ray, the vet finally made a conclusive diagnosis: Ladoo had incurable congestive heart disease. The best I could do was manage the signs and symptoms when they occurred. The vet also said, "She has to be on medication for life.

In the many days after 11th of January 2013, I wondered about how long that 'for life' would be. Some vets said three years; other people said four months. A lady at the clinic said her dog was on the same medication and had been on it for five years. At night, with Ladoo resting her head in my lap, struggling to sleep, I surfed the Net to understand this condition – congestive heart disease – and find treatment options and suitable medication for her. And I learnt the sense of hopelessness a mother feels when her child is ill.

One night during this hellish time, neither of us slept. Ladoo's girth became larger by the hour, filling up with fluid. Her skin was painfully taut which made it impossible for her to sit. Her laboured breathing made it hard for her to lie down, walk or rest. While we lay on the bed and I waited for morning to come so that I could rush her to the vet, I held her close and did the only thing that came to mind: I recited the Maha Mitrunjaya mantra, which Hindus believe wards off death.

Over the course of the next few weeks, various things were said to me from "You'll have to accept it when the end comes," and "Don't get too attached so that you're not hurt." The worst thing said was, "After all, she's already nine. She is a dog, you know." During intense moments, I consoled myself that since Ladoo was part of a family whose members have defied heart disease and lived much longer than expected, she, too, would live for a long time.

As it turned out, Ladoo lived for 78 days after that first attack. During that time, our lives can be summed up in part of a text message I sent to a friend while I waited at a doctor's clinic:

Can you say a prayer for Ladoo, please? She's filling up with fluid again & when the vet took some out to send to test, there was blood in it. The veterinary nurse began to cry. I'm being prepared for the worst. ... She's weak & she's scared. ... I can't even carry her because that presses on her chest. In all honesty, I'm wondering if she'll still be alive when I go home.

Throughout the day on 29th of March 2013, the air was still and it was stiflingly hot and humid. When I took Ladoo out to pee, she went down and couldn't come back up. She could no longer walk. I didn't say a word. Instead, I carried her back inside and arranged the bed downstairs for us. I prayed she would settle and get some rest.

By 9.45 p.m., my father had gone up to sleep and I was lying on the bed with Ladoo by my side. My mother kept us company for a while. Then, at 9.53 p.m., I saw that her tongue was pale and knew something was wrong.

While my mother went to call my father, I rushed to feed Ladoo some juice.

My parents say that as they made their way downstairs, they could hear me screaming. I don't remember this. What I do remember is trying everything from CPR to beating her chest to save my dog. When I didn't know what else to do, I held her close and hugged her. Then, in a manner that was ever so tender, my father put his hand on my back and said, "Neeta, she's gone. See, there's no heartbeat." That's when Ladoo's head fell on my chest, lifeless. Softly, my mother said, "She's gone." And I started to cry.

Once the decision was made to bury Ladoo in my parents' garden, my mother phoned the gardener and he agreed to be at our house by 7.30 a.m. By 11 p.m., Ladoo was clean, wrapped up and 'lying in state' in our hall. With the Maha Mitrunjaya mantra playing in the background, I kept my baby company on her last night with me. I told my parents to go to sleep as they had to work the next day.

I think my parents had the fright of their lives when they came downstairs at one point in the night and saw me lying down on the floor, next to Ladoo with my hand on her body. I explained to them that this dog would wake me up in the middle of the night to come into bed because she was frightened. She might have her face turned away, but part of her body had to be touching mine all through the night. How could I leave her completely alone now?

After my parents returned to bed, during the quiet hours, I thought about all the joy Ladoo had given me. Suddenly, I remembered what day it was: Ladoo had chosen to die on a very good day – 29th of March 2013 was Good Friday.

The plan in the morning was for my mother and I to go to the temple as we normally do then be back in time for Ladoo's burial. Ah Chai, our gardener, turned up earlier than expected. Once we found the spot for Ladoo's final resting place, Ah Chai got started. In no time at all, the hole was deep enough and I placed her body with her head facing north so that the sun would always shine on her face.

Ladoo's final resting place.

At the temple, something unexpected happened. Usually, I light a small ghee lamp before saying my prayers. This time, when I asked for a ghee lamp, of his own volition, the priest gave me a huge ghee lamp and said it was a 'Moksha Deepum' lamp. I continue to believe that the Divine had a hand that day in making me light a lamp for Ladoo that symbolises the liberation of the soul.

What took me by surprise was the response I received once news of Ladoo's death spread. There was Mr. Lim, my contractor, who insisted I remain composed as Ladoo wouldn't want to see me sad. Paramjyoti, the newspaper delivery guy, rang me at midnight and half-scolded me with, "How did this happen?"

It was impossible to understand what Precy was saying when she called from the Philippines because she couldn't stop crying long enough to speak. I had to insist that Uncle Rao come inside the house because I didn't want to cry in the middle of the road when I read the words of a condolence card he delivered. I marvelled that the hibiscus that Aunty Jeroo brought from her garden and laid on Ladoo's grave was still red five days after Ladoo died.

Joanna, my writer friend from the US lit a candle charged with Reiki and put her snowflake obsidian bracelet around the candle, as part of her prayer for Ladoo's safe passage from this world to heaven or to her next life. Eight-year-old Raj from Seremban promised to give me a hug to comfort me when we next met and six-year-old Aaryan ordered me to get another dog, "exactly like Ladoo; and you must call her Ladoo also." How could I explain to this sweet child that Ladoo cannot be replaced? Instead, I said I would do as he wanted.

I told Ravi, Ladoo's vet, what Aaryan said and added that I don't feel the time is right as yet to bring another dog into my life. For nine years, my life has been defined as 'Aneeta and Ladoo'. As I said, in Ladoo's eyes, you were coming to see her. Ravi quietly responded, "Aneeta, for nine years, it's not been 'Aneeta and Ladoo'; it's been 'Ladoo and Aneeta'". Point taken.

Even in death, Ladoo has taught me a lesson. A few years ago, my parents and I had a misunderstanding with some friends. When a close family member of theirs died, my parents insisted on visiting them to express their condolences. Since our friendship had ended, I remember asking, "Why?" Now, I know the answer because one of my friendships ended a while ago. This friend was one of Ladoo's favourite people. In fact, a week before she died, I said his name and she wagged her tail, not from side to side, but round and round, ecstatic. When Ladoo died, I swallowed my pride and texted him to relay the sad news. I've tried to understand, analyse and comprehend his deafening silence to no avail. The lesson is this: when someone dies, an offer of condolence to the next of kin certainly comforts them; more importantly, it honours the dead.

The evening before I left Alor Star to return to my flat in the city, I stood by Ladoo's grave and said goodbye. I told her I had brought her home to rest in peace and asked her to watch over my parents while I was away. I once wrote that when my sweet dachshund dies, a part of me will die with her. That is true, but I take comfort in the words in an email another writer friend, Susan, sent me: "The pain and sadness will ease with time, but the bond will remain forever."

Author's Note

This book started out as a blog because I wanted to keep a record of Ladoo's antics when she was still alive. It became an eBook and now, this. The aim has been to capture the stories of this dachshund who came into my life when I needed her most: I'd not only left my job, I'd walked away from a career I'd spent years working towards. Forging a new career as a writer has been tough, but the unconditional love Ladoo gave me soothed my soul and made the journey bearable.

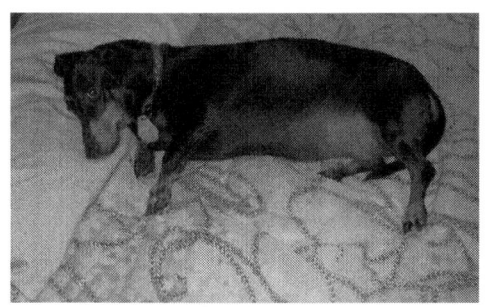

"Oh dear!"

This photo, one of the last few taken of Ladoo, is an all-time family favourite. It says everything about my dachshund. One afternoon, when we were lying down and Ladoo was at her usual spot at the foot of the bed, I left the room for a few seconds. When I returned, I found her in this position. The look in her eyes and the tail between the legs shows she knows she's guilty of doing something she isn't supposed to. The head on the pillow says, "But Mummy, I want to be close to you. To share with you, Mummy." The left paw gingerly reaching out is a nervous invitation to me. How could I possibly be angry with her?

It is true that before Ladoo, I had a carefree life. It is also true that while Ladoo was with me, I stepped onto a plane only twice or thrice as I didn't want to leave her with strangers. Instead, I took Ladoo with me on all my holidays.

People have called these sacrifices and said that I've missed out on doing 'things'. When they've explained what these 'things' are, they pale in comparison to the joy Ladoo has brought into my life and the lives of the people around us – I've seen her make grumpy people laugh; I've watched her offer comfort to friends who are unable to overcome their grief; I've seen her bring out the tenderness in shy or reticent people; I've felt safe when she sits with me in the car and warns approaching hooligans not to come any further with her growl. I hope that from these stories, you have come to learn a little about a much-loved dog.

Now that we've come to the end, I have two requests to make: first, if you have any comments, please feel free to write to me at editor@howtotellagreatstory.com. Second, please say a prayer for the repose of Ladoo's soul. Thank you.

Aneeta Sundararaj
August 2013

Back Cover

The 12 stories in this collection are a personal account of the antics of my exuberant dachshund, Ladoo. While most of the stories are about what Ladoo gets up to, some of them are about how ludicrous humans can be about dogs.

Above all, these stories show that if you open your heart to a dog, it will give you its whole heart in return. Here's something Aneeta wrote that appeared in a story posted online that says it all: "My mother says that Ladoo must have done some good karma to be loved this much. In fact, I think the opposite is true: I must have done some good karma for the many blessings and joy she's brought me. God give me strength for I know that when my sweet dachshund dies, a part of me will die with her."

Made in the USA
Middletown, DE
26 July 2024